Serving In The Shadows

Joshua Rhoades

Published by Joshua Paul Rhoades, 2024.

SERVING IN THE SHADOWS

First edition. October 6, 2024.

ISBN: 979-8227771001

Written by Joshua Rhoades.

Also by Joshua Rhoades

Courage Under Fire: David's Stand On The Battlefield
Jonah's Journey: Voices Of Redemption And Lessons In Obedience
The Furnace Of Faith: 12 Principles From The Heat Of Faith
Whispers of Hope: Inspiring Stories of Men's Prayers In Scripture
Frontier Legends: The Oregon Dream
Elijah: A Beacon Of Boldness
HOOK, LINE & SAVIOUR - Faith Reflections from Fishing
Driven By Faith: Motor Racing Inspired Christian Life
30 Day Devotional - Bold and Strong- Coffee Devotions for a
Courageous Christian Walk
Authentic Christianity: The Heart of Old Time Religion
Consider The Ant - God's Tiny Preachers
Flee Fornication: The Plea For Purity
Renewed Hope- How to Find Encouragement in God
Sounding The Call - The Voice of Conviction
The Altar - Where Heaven Meets Earth
The Bible's Battlefields- Timeless Lessons from Ancient Wars
The Sacred Art of Silence - How Silence Speaks in Scripture
Under Fire- The Sanctity of the Traditional Biblical Home
Who Is on the Lord's Side? A Call to Righteousness
What Is Truth? - From Skepticism to Submission
First and Goal- Faith and Football Fundamentals
From Dugout to Devotion- Spiritual Lessons from Baseball
Par for the Course- Faith and Fairways
The Believer's Pace- Tools for Running Life's Marathon

The Calling and Greatness of John the Baptist
For Such a Time Esther's Courageous Stand
From Brokenness To Beauty Written By The Pen of Grace
The Ultimate Guide to Massive Action- From Plans to Reality
A Heart Of Conviction
Serving In The Shadows

Dedication

To you, the quiet warrior, the steadfast servant, this book is dedicated. You, who may often feel unseen, unheard, and unnoticed as you go about your work, let me assure you—your service matters deeply. The world may not applaud your efforts, you may not stand in the spotlight, but the work you do in the shadows, the care you provide in the background, and the sacrifices you make in silence are powerful beyond measure. It takes immense strength to serve without recognition, to give your heart and soul to a cause, to people, or to a purpose, knowing that there may be no applause at the end of the day. But you do it anyway, because you believe in something greater. You believe that there is value in faithfulness, that there is beauty in humility, and that the quiet dedication of a servant's heart can change lives, heal wounds, and shine light in places that desperately need it.

This dedication is for the one who lifts others up, supports them without seeking praise, and works behind the scenes to make things happen. It's for the mother who sacrifices her dreams to raise her children, the caregiver who quietly tends to the sick, the teacher who pours into students without expectation of thanks, the friend who listens when no one else does, and the leader who leads without demanding attention. It's for every person who understands that true greatness lies not in recognition, but in the quiet, steady work of love, service, and faith.

In the shadows, your character is forged. In the shadows, your spirit is refined. And though others may not see, God sees. He sees every moment of sacrifice, every tear shed in silence, every act of kindness done without expectation. He sees the battles you fight quietly, the burdens you carry alone, and the faithfulness you show when no one else is watching. And He values you, more than you could ever imagine. You are not invisible to Him. You are treasured.

To you, who serve in the shadows, I dedicate this book as a reminder that your service is seen, your heart is cherished, and your impact is immeasurable. Keep going, for your work is not in vain. You are making a difference in ways you may never fully realize. You are building something beautiful, something eternal, and one day, the quiet work of your hands, done in faith, will echo in ways that far surpass what the world could ever offer. Thank you for your service. Your faithfulness in the shadows is what truly lights up the world.

Introduction

"Serving in the Shadows" is about those who work quietly, faithfully, and often unnoticed, yet make a profound impact on the world. It is for the countless people whose contributions may never be acknowledged in public but are crucial to the success of others and the larger mission they serve. Throughout history and in everyday life, these individuals have carried out their tasks with dedication, commitment, and humility, knowing that the true measure of success is not in recognition or praise, but in the act of service itself. The Bible offers numerous examples of such individuals who served in the shadows—people who didn't seek fame or acclaim but played critical roles in God's plan. From Bezalel, the craftsman who used his skills to build the tabernacle, to Andrew, who quietly brought his brother Peter to Jesus, these individuals remind us that it is not always the visible, well-known figures who make the most significant contributions, but often those who work diligently behind the scenes.

This book seeks to explore the lives and lessons of these biblical figures and many others who exemplified what it means to serve with humility and faithfulness. Bezalel, for instance, was filled with the Spirit of God and gifted with wisdom, understanding, and skill to craft the sacred furnishings of the tabernacle. His work was not in the public eye, but it laid the foundation for the worship of God among the Israelites. Without Bezalel's craftsmanship, the tabernacle—where God's presence would dwell—would not have been constructed. He didn't seek recognition for his work, but he used his God-given talents to glorify God and benefit the people of Israel. Similarly, the unnamed servant girl in the story of Naaman, the Syrian commander, played a pivotal role in his miraculous healing. Though she was a captive and seemingly insignificant, her quiet suggestion to seek out the prophet Elisha led to Naaman's encounter with the one true God. These stories show us that even the smallest, most unnoticed acts of service can have far-reaching and eternal consequences.

Serving in the shadows requires a special kind of strength. It takes humility to work without recognition, courage to continue in the face of hardship, and faith to believe that what you're doing matters, even if no one else seems to notice. In a world that often celebrates only the loudest voices and the most visible achievements, those who serve in the shadows remind us that true greatness is found in quiet, consistent acts of love and service. These acts might not attract attention, but they build the foundations upon which lives, communities, and even nations are transformed. They are the glue that holds things together, the invisible threads that weave the fabric of society, faith, and family.

This book also seeks to encourage those who feel unseen or unappreciated in their work. You may not be in the spotlight, and your efforts may go unnoticed by the world, but they are never unnoticed by God. Just as God saw the faithfulness of individuals like Epaphroditus, who risked his life to serve Paul in prison, and Barnabas, the "Son of Encouragement," who uplifted others and supported Paul's ministry, He sees your faithfulness. He sees the sacrifices you make, the hard work you put in, and the love you pour out, even when it goes unacknowledged by others. The Bible reminds us repeatedly that God values the heart of a servant, and it is often those who serve quietly and faithfully who make the most lasting impact. Jesus Himself said, "But many that are first shall be last; and the last shall be first" (Matthew 19:30, KJV). Those who serve without seeking recognition are honored by God, who sees the hidden work done in His name.

"Serving in the Shadows" also addresses the emotional and spiritual challenges that come with this kind of service. It's not always easy to keep going when it feels like no one appreciates your work. Feelings of discouragement, loneliness, or even resentment can creep in when we feel overlooked or taken for granted. But this book offers hope and encouragement for those moments, reminding us that God is always with us, strengthening us and giving us purpose. He calls us to a life of service, not for the applause of men, but for His glory. And when we serve in the shadows, we are following the example of Jesus, who came not to be served but to serve, and to give His life as a ransom for many (Mark 10:45, KJV).

Through the lives of biblical figures and their stories of quiet service, we learn that true greatness is found in the humble act of serving others without expectation of recognition. It's about putting others before ourselves, being faithful in the small things, and trusting that God will use our efforts for His glory. Whether it's Jonathan's armor-bearer, who loyally followed his leader into battle, or Tychicus, who served as a faithful messenger for Paul, carrying letters that would become part of the New Testament, each of these individuals shows us that there is no task too small when done for the Lord. Their stories remind us that God uses ordinary people doing ordinary things to accomplish extraordinary purposes.

In today's world, where success is often measured by fame, wealth, and power, "Serving in the Shadows" offers a refreshing and countercultural message. It reminds us that our worth is not determined by how much attention we receive or how many people praise us for our work. Our worth comes from being faithful stewards of the gifts and opportunities God has given us, no matter how big or small. And when we serve in the shadows, we are part of something much bigger than ourselves—we are part of God's redemptive work in the world.

So, as you read this book, I invite you to consider your own life and your own acts of service. You may feel like you are working in obscurity, unnoticed by others, but know that your work is seen and valued by the One who matters most. Whether you are raising children, caring for a loved one, working in a job that feels thankless, or serving in a ministry that doesn't bring you recognition, remember that you are making a difference. Just as Bezalel, Andrew, Naaman's servant girl, and so many others did, you are playing a vital role in God's plan. Your service in the shadows is significant, and God is using it in ways you may never fully understand.

"Serving in the Shadows" is not just a collection of stories; it's an invitation to embrace a life of humble, faithful service, knowing that in God's kingdom, it is often those who are unseen by the world who make the greatest impact. As you reflect on the lives of these biblical characters, may you be encouraged and inspired to continue serving with joy, knowing that God sees you, loves you, and honors your faithful work. You are not forgotten. You are not invisible. You are serving the King, and that is a privilege beyond measure.

Chapter 1 – The Silent Servant

Andrew, the silent servant, is a powerful example of what it means to serve in the shadows. In John 1:40-41, we see that Andrew was one of the first to follow Jesus, but unlike his brother Peter, who became one of the most well-known apostles, Andrew's role was quieter, more behind-the-scenes. However, his service was no less important. Andrew did not seek the spotlight or try to draw attention to himself; instead, he focused on bringing others to Jesus. One of his most significant acts was bringing Peter, his brother, to meet Jesus, which would lead to Peter becoming a central figure in the early church. Though Andrew is often overshadowed by Peter, it was his quiet, faithful actions that helped set the stage for Peter's future leadership. Andrew didn't need to be the one in the spotlight; he was content to serve by helping others find Jesus. This kind of service is often overlooked in our world, where recognition and fame are highly valued, but Andrew's story shows us that serving in the shadows can be just as, if not more, impactful than being in the spotlight.

What makes Andrew's service so remarkable is that it was done with a humble heart. He didn't seek praise or validation from others; his only focus was on connecting people with Jesus. Andrew's actions paved the way for many others to follow Christ, including Peter, who would go on to preach to thousands and lead the early church. Yet, Andrew wasn't concerned with receiving credit for his role in Peter's journey. His quiet service reminds us that God sees and values all acts of obedience, even when they are done without recognition. In fact, many of the most meaningful acts of service happen behind the scenes, where no one is watching except God. Andrew's life teaches us that serving in the shadows requires humility and faith. It requires trusting that what we do matters, even if it doesn't bring us fame or attention.

Andrew's service was also impactful because it was consistent. Throughout the Gospels, we see Andrew quietly bringing people to Jesus. He was one of the disciples who found the boy with the loaves and fishes and brought him to Jesus, leading to the miracle of feeding the five thousand. He didn't perform the miracle himself, but his role in facilitating it was crucial. Again, Andrew was content to play a supporting role, trusting that Jesus would do the rest. His willingness to bring people to Jesus, whether it was his own brother or a young boy with a small offering, shows us the importance of being faithful in small things. Andrew wasn't focused on making a name for himself; he was focused on connecting people to the one who could truly change their lives.

In today's world, we often feel pressure to be seen and acknowledged for our work, but Andrew's example shows us that the most important service is often done quietly. Serving in the shadows means being willing to do the work, even if no one notices or gives us credit. It means being content with the knowledge that God sees our efforts, even when others don't. Andrew didn't need human praise to validate his service; he knew that his work was valuable because it was part of God's plan. This kind of service requires a deep sense of purpose and a willingness to let go of the need for recognition. It's not always easy to serve without being seen, but Andrew's life shows us that this kind of service is incredibly meaningful.

Andrew's quiet service also paved the way for future leaders. By bringing Peter to Jesus, Andrew played a crucial role in the development of the early church. Peter went on to become one of the most influential apostles, preaching to thousands and helping to establish the Christian faith. But without Andrew's initial introduction, Peter might never have met Jesus. Andrew's service in the shadows set the stage for Peter's public ministry, showing us that behind every great leader, there are often people who serve quietly and faithfully, helping to support and guide them along the way. Andrew's example reminds us that even when we aren't the ones in the spotlight, our work can have a profound impact on others.

Serving in the shadows doesn't mean that our work is less important. In fact, Andrew's story shows us that quiet, humble service can have a lasting impact that goes far beyond what we can see. Andrew's life may not have been filled with the same dramatic moments as Peter's, but his faithful service laid the foundation for much of what came later. His story challenges us to think about how we can serve in ways that might not bring us recognition but still contribute to God's greater plan. Whether it's bringing someone to Jesus, offering a small act of kindness, or faithfully doing the work that God has called us to, serving in the shadows is a powerful way to live out our faith.

In conclusion, Andrew's role as the silent servant teaches us that serving in the shadows is not about seeking recognition or fame, but about being faithful to God's call. His quiet, yet impactful, service paved the way for many others to follow Christ, including his brother Peter, who became a central figure in the early church. Andrew's story reminds us that the most meaningful acts of service are often the ones done without fanfare, behind the scenes, where only God sees. Serving in the shadows requires humility, faith, and a willingness to let go of the need for human praise. It's about trusting that God values our service, even when no one else notices, and that our quiet acts of obedience can have a lasting impact on others. Just like Andrew, we can serve faithfully, knowing that our work, whether seen or unseen, is an important part of God's plan.

Chapter 2 – The Selfless Supporter

Epaphroditus is a great example of someone who served in the shadows, doing important work without seeking attention or fame, as shown in Philippians 2:25-30. He was not a well-known figure like some of the other early Christians, but the way he served is incredibly significant. Epaphroditus was sent by the church in Philippi to bring aid to Paul while he was in prison. This was not an easy task, as traveling in those days was dangerous, and there were many risks involved, especially when it came to associating with someone who was imprisoned for his faith. But Epaphroditus was willing to take those risks because he cared about helping Paul and supporting the work of spreading the gospel. He didn't let fear or concern for his own safety stop him from serving others. His actions show that serving in the shadows often means putting the needs of others ahead of your own, even when it's difficult or dangerous.

Epaphroditus's service was selfless. He wasn't doing this for recognition or praise; he was simply doing what needed to be done. In fact, he became very sick during his journey and nearly died, but he kept going because he knew how important it was to bring help to Paul. His willingness to sacrifice his own health and comfort for the sake of others is a powerful example of what it means to serve selflessly. Paul was deeply appreciative of what Epaphroditus did, and in his letter to the Philippians, he made sure to acknowledge the significance of Epaphroditus's sacrifice. Even though Epaphroditus wasn't seeking recognition, Paul made sure that his service didn't go unnoticed. This shows that while serving in the shadows may not always bring public praise, those who are truly paying attention will recognize and appreciate the sacrifices that are made.

Serving in the shadows, as Epaphroditus did, also requires a deep sense of commitment. It's easy to serve when things are going well, or when there's a lot of recognition involved, but Epaphroditus's example shows that true service often happens when things are hard. He didn't give up when he got sick; he kept going because he was committed to helping Paul and doing what was needed. This kind of dedication is a hallmark of serving in the shadows. It means staying focused on the mission, even when it's challenging or uncomfortable. Epaphroditus could have turned back or decided that it wasn't worth the risk, but he didn't. He pushed through because he knew that his service mattered.

Another important aspect of Epaphroditus's story is that he was willing to serve in a supporting role. He wasn't the one out front, preaching to large crowds or leading a church. Instead, he was the one who brought aid to someone else who was doing that work. But his role was just as important. Without people like Epaphroditus, the work of people like Paul wouldn't have been possible. This is what it means to serve in the shadows – to do the work that may not be as visible but is still vital to the overall mission. Epaphroditus didn't need to be in the spotlight to know that what he was doing mattered. He understood that supporting others is a crucial part of the work of spreading the gospel.

Paul's recognition of Epaphroditus in his letter to the Philippians shows that serving in the shadows doesn't go unnoticed by God or by those who truly value what matters. Paul made sure to tell the Philippians to honor Epaphroditus and people like him, who risk their lives for the sake of the gospel. This is a reminder that even though serving in the shadows might not bring fame or public recognition, it is still incredibly important. The sacrifices made by people like Epaphroditus are what allow the work of the kingdom to move forward, and those sacrifices are deeply valued by God.

Epaphroditus's story also shows us that serving in the shadows can have a big impact, even if it doesn't seem like it at the time. He wasn't doing anything flashy or attention-grabbing; he was simply bringing aid to someone who needed it. But that small act of service had a huge impact on Paul and his ability to continue his ministry. Sometimes, we think that serving in the shadows means that our work doesn't matter as much, but Epaphroditus's example shows us that even the smallest acts of service can make a big difference. When we serve selflessly, without worrying about whether or not we'll get credit for it, we can trust that God will use our efforts in ways we might not even realize.

In conclusion, Epaphroditus is a powerful example of what it means to serve in the shadows. He wasn't seeking fame or recognition; he was simply doing what needed to be done to support someone else. His selfless service, even in the face of illness and danger, shows us the importance of putting others before ourselves and staying committed to the mission, no matter what challenges come our way. Paul's acknowledgment of Epaphroditus's sacrifice reminds us that even though serving in the shadows might not bring public recognition, it is deeply valued by those who understand the true nature of service. Epaphroditus's story teaches us that serving in the shadows is not about being in the spotlight; it's about being faithful, committed, and willing to make sacrifices for the sake of others. Even though we may not always see the immediate impact of our service, we can trust that God sees and values every act of selflessness, just as Paul valued the service of Epaphroditus. Serving in the shadows might not bring fame, but it brings something much more important: the satisfaction of knowing that we are making a difference in the lives of others, even when no one else is watching.

Chapter 3 – The Submissive Servant

Ananias, the submissive servant, is an excellent example of what it means to serve in the shadows, as shown in Acts 9:10-18. Ananias was a faithful follower of God, but he wasn't someone who was widely known or celebrated in the early church. His story is brief, yet it holds a powerful message about obedience, trust, and serving without needing recognition. When God called Ananias to go and heal Saul, who later became known as Paul, Ananias had every reason to be afraid. Saul was known for persecuting Christians, and many believers had suffered because of him. Ananias could have easily let fear keep him from answering God's call. After all, approaching someone like Saul seemed dangerous and even life-threatening. However, despite his fears, Ananias chose to submit to God's command. His willingness to step out in faith and serve, even when it was difficult, is what makes his service so remarkable. Ananias wasn't focused on what others would think or whether he would be praised for his actions. He was simply committed to obeying God, no matter the cost.

What's amazing about Ananias's role is that, though he served quietly and without fanfare, his actions had an enormous impact on the future of Christianity. Saul, whom Ananias was sent to heal, would go on to become the Apostle Paul, one of the most influential figures in the New Testament. Paul's writings and missionary work helped spread the gospel throughout the world, and his letters continue to be a vital part of Christian teaching today. Yet, it was Ananias, the submissive servant, who played a critical role in Paul's conversion. By obeying God's call to heal Saul's blindness and baptize him, Ananias helped set Paul on the path that would lead to his incredible ministry. This shows that even though Ananias wasn't the one in the spotlight, his service behind the scenes was essential to God's plan. Serving in the shadows often means playing a supporting role, but that doesn't make the service any less valuable or important.

Ananias's story also teaches us about the importance of trusting God, even when His plans don't make sense to us. When God told Ananias to go to Saul, Ananias initially hesitated because he knew how dangerous Saul had been to Christians. But God reassured him that Saul was a chosen instrument who would carry His name before the Gentiles, kings, and the people of Israel. Despite his fear, Ananias trusted that God knew what He was doing, and he submitted to His will. This kind of trust is key to serving in the shadows. It requires us to let go of our own understanding and rely on God's wisdom, knowing that He sees the bigger picture even when we don't. Ananias's obedience shows that sometimes, serving in the shadows means stepping into uncomfortable or even risky situations because we trust that God's plan is always good.

Another important aspect of Ananias's service is his humility. He didn't demand recognition or praise for his role in Saul's conversion. In fact, after his brief encounter with Saul, Ananias disappears from the narrative, and we don't hear about him again. This shows that Ananias wasn't concerned with receiving credit for his actions. He was simply focused on being obedient to God and doing what was asked of him. Serving in the shadows often means being content with the knowledge that God sees and values our service, even if no one else does. Ananias's humility is a reminder that the true reward for our service comes from knowing that we have been faithful to God's calling, not from receiving praise or recognition from others.

Ananias's willingness to serve also had a ripple effect that extended far beyond what he could have imagined. By healing Saul and helping him become a follower of Christ, Ananias played a part in the spread of the gospel to countless people. Paul's ministry would go on to impact thousands of lives, and his writings continue to influence Christians around the world today. Yet, none of that would have been possible without Ananias's quiet, obedient service. This shows that serving in the shadows can have far-reaching effects, even when we don't see the immediate results of our efforts. Sometimes, the impact of our service isn't fully realized until much later, but that doesn't make it any less significant.

In conclusion, Ananias, the submissive servant, teaches us that serving in the shadows is about obedience, trust, humility, and faith. His willingness to submit to God's calling, even when it was frightening, led to one of the most important conversions in Christian history. Ananias's story reminds us that serving in the shadows doesn't mean our work is less valuable or important; it simply means that we are willing to serve without needing recognition or praise. Like Ananias, we are called to trust God's plan, even when it doesn't make sense to us, and to be faithful in whatever He asks us to do. Serving in the shadows requires humility, as it often means playing a supporting role, but it is through this kind of quiet, faithful service that God's work is accomplished. Ananias's example shows us that even the smallest acts of obedience can have a profound impact on the lives of others and on God's kingdom as a whole. Though his time in the spotlight was brief, Ananias's legacy lives on through the life and ministry of Paul, reminding us that serving in the shadows can lead to great things when we submit to God's will.

Chapter 4 – The Steadfast Sentry

Mordecai, the steadfast sentry, is a powerful example of serving in the shadows, as shown in Esther 2:21-23. Mordecai played a crucial role in the book of Esther, yet he is not the one who often receives the spotlight or recognition. He served faithfully and quietly as a gatekeeper for the king, always remaining vigilant in his position. Mordecai's service was not glamorous or attention-seeking, but it was essential. He was dedicated to his duties, and his vigilance eventually uncovered a plot to assassinate the king. Mordecai could have easily chosen to ignore this plot, but his sense of duty and faithfulness led him to report it, saving the king's life. Though Mordecai didn't seek reward or recognition for his actions, his service was recorded in the royal chronicles, and this act would later play a pivotal role in the salvation of the Jewish people. His steadfast commitment to doing the right thing, even when no one was watching, is the essence of what it means to serve in the shadows.

Mordecai's story is a reminder that serving in the shadows often means being faithful in the small, everyday tasks that might seem insignificant but can have a far-reaching impact. As a gatekeeper, Mordecai's job wasn't one that brought him fame or power, but he took it seriously and performed it with diligence. He didn't know at the time how important his vigilance would become, but his faithfulness in this seemingly small role ended up playing a major part in the survival of his people. Serving in the shadows means understanding that every act of service, no matter how small or unseen, is valuable in God's eyes. Mordecai's story shows us that it's not always the people in the spotlight who make the biggest difference. Sometimes, it's the quiet, steady work of those in the background that changes the course of history.

What makes Mordecai's service even more remarkable is that he didn't seek personal gain or recognition for his actions. After saving the king's life, he wasn't immediately rewarded, and he didn't demand recognition. He continued to serve faithfully as a gatekeeper, content to do his work without expecting praise. This kind of humility is a key part of serving in the shadows. It requires being willing to do what's right simply because it's the right thing to do, not because of the rewards or acknowledgment we might receive. Mordecai's humility and dedication to his duty are a powerful example of what it means to serve selflessly, trusting that God sees and values our efforts, even if no one else does.

Mordecai's steadfastness and faithfulness didn't just save the king's life; they also played a critical role in the salvation of the Jewish people. Later in the story, when Haman, one of the king's officials, plotted to destroy the Jews, Mordecai again took action, this time by encouraging his cousin Esther to use her position as queen to intervene on behalf of their people. Mordecai's wisdom and guidance helped Esther find the courage to speak up, and through their combined efforts, Haman's plot was thwarted, and the Jewish people were saved. Mordecai's role in this story is a reminder that serving in the shadows doesn't mean being passive or uninvolved. It means being ready and willing to act when the time comes, even if it means working behind the scenes. Mordecai's faithfulness in his everyday duties prepared him for the moment when he would need to take a stand and help save his people.

Another important aspect of Mordecai's story is his trust in God's plan. When Esther expressed fear about approaching the king to plead for their people, Mordecai reminded her that she might have been placed in her position "for such a time as this" (Esther 4:14). Mordecai believed that God had a purpose for Esther's rise to power, and he trusted that God was working behind the scenes to bring about His plan for the salvation of the Jewish people. Serving in the shadows often requires this kind of trust. We may not always see how our actions fit into the bigger picture, but we can trust that God is using our faithfulness in ways we might not even realize. Mordecai's unwavering faith in God's plan allowed him to serve with confidence, even when the future seemed uncertain.

In the end, Mordecai's faithfulness and service were rewarded. After Haman's plot was uncovered, the king honored Mordecai by giving him Haman's position of power, and Mordecai became a leader who was highly respected and beloved by his people. But Mordecai's story isn't about seeking power or recognition. It's about serving faithfully, humbly, and with a steadfast commitment to doing what's right, no matter the circumstances. Mordecai's rise to power was not something he sought for himself; it was the result of his faithful service in the shadows, and it came about in God's perfect timing.

Mordecai's story teaches us that serving in the shadows often involves patience, humility, and a willingness to trust that God is working through our efforts, even when we don't see immediate results. It's about being faithful in the everyday tasks and responsibilities that God has given us, knowing that He has a purpose for everything we do. Mordecai didn't know when he uncovered the assassination plot that it would later play a key role in saving his people, but he remained faithful to his duty, trusting that God was in control. Serving in the shadows means being willing to play a supporting role, understanding that our service is valuable, even if it's not always visible to others.

In conclusion, Mordecai's story as the steadfast sentry shows us that serving in the shadows is about being faithful, humble, and steadfast in whatever role God has given us. His vigilance and commitment to doing what was right, even when no one was watching, saved the king's life and, eventually, the lives of the Jewish people. Mordecai didn't seek recognition or reward for his actions, but he trusted that God had a plan, and he remained faithful to his duties, no matter how small or unseen they seemed. His story is a powerful reminder that serving in the shadows can have a lasting impact, and that God sees and values every act of service, no matter how hidden it may be. Mordecai's faithfulness in the background prepared him for the moment when God would use him to help save His people, showing us that even the quiet, behind-the-scenes work of those who serve in the shadows can change the course of history.

Chapter 5 – The Secret Saviors

Shiphrah and Puah, the secret saviors, exemplify what it means to serve in the shadows through their courageous and hidden service, as shown in Exodus 1:15-21. These two Hebrew midwives are remarkable for their bravery and faithfulness during a time of great danger for the Hebrew people. Pharaoh, the ruler of Egypt, had ordered that all Hebrew baby boys be killed at birth to control the growing population of Israelites. This was a cruel and horrifying command, but Shiphrah and Puah, tasked with carrying out this order, chose to defy Pharaoh in secret. Instead of killing the newborn boys as they had been instructed, they made the courageous decision to preserve the lives of these innocent children, risking their own safety in the process. Their work was hidden from the public eye, and they didn't receive recognition or praise for their actions at the time, but their quiet defiance and faithfulness to God saved countless lives, including the life of Moses, who would grow up to lead the Israelites out of slavery in Egypt and into freedom.

Shiphrah and Puah's actions show the incredible power of serving in the shadows. They didn't act for recognition or personal gain, but out of a deep sense of compassion and a fear of God. They knew that what they were doing was dangerous, yet they were willing to risk everything to do what was right. In choosing to secretly save the Hebrew boys, they demonstrated immense courage, even though their actions went against the most powerful man in the land, Pharaoh. Their story reminds us that serving in the shadows often means doing what is right, even when it's not easy or safe. It's about standing up for justice and protecting others, even when no one else is watching. Shiphrah and Puah didn't need public acknowledgment to motivate them. They were driven by their faith and their commitment to preserving life, trusting that God would protect and bless them for their courageous actions.

What makes Shiphrah and Puah's service so extraordinary is that it wasn't just a one-time act of bravery; it was an ongoing commitment to quietly and faithfully defy an unjust order. They continued to deliver Hebrew babies safely, hiding their actions from Pharaoh and protecting the future of their people. Their story highlights the importance of perseverance in serving in the shadows. It's not always about grand, visible acts of heroism, but rather about the consistent, faithful efforts to do what is right, day after day, even when it seems like no one notices. Shiphrah and Puah didn't know that their actions would one day be recorded in Scripture or that they would be remembered as heroes. They simply did what needed to be done, trusting that their efforts mattered, even if they were never recognized by others.

Another powerful aspect of Shiphrah and Puah's service is that it wasn't just about protecting individual lives, but about preserving the future of an entire nation. By saving the Hebrew boys, they ensured the survival of the Israelite people, who would later be freed from slavery through God's deliverance. One of the babies they saved was Moses, who would grow up to become the leader and deliverer of Israel. Without the quiet, hidden service of Shiphrah and Puah, Moses might never have survived, and the history of the Israelites could have been very different. Their story shows that serving in the shadows can have a profound impact, even if we don't see the immediate results of our efforts. Sometimes, the full importance of our service is only revealed later, but that doesn't make it any less significant.

Shiphrah and Puah's faithfulness also teaches us about the importance of fearing God rather than fearing people. Pharaoh was a powerful and dangerous ruler, and disobeying his orders could have cost them their lives. Yet, Shiphrah and Puah feared God more than they feared Pharaoh. They understood that obeying God's commands and protecting innocent lives was far more important than submitting to an unjust human ruler. This kind of faith and trust in God is essential to serving in the shadows. It requires the courage to stand firm in our convictions, even when it means going against the expectations or demands of others. Shiphrah and Puah didn't know what would happen to them as a result of their defiance, but they trusted that God would honor their faithfulness, and He did. The Bible tells us that God blessed them for their actions, giving them families of their own. Their story reminds us that when we serve faithfully in the shadows, God sees our efforts, and He rewards those who act with courage and integrity, even when the world does not.

In conclusion, Shiphrah and Puah's story as the secret saviors teaches us that serving in the shadows is about courage, faithfulness, and a deep commitment to doing what is right, even when it's difficult or dangerous. Their hidden service preserved the lives of many Hebrew children, including Moses, the future deliverer of Israel, and their actions had a lasting impact on the future of their people. Shiphrah and Puah didn't seek recognition or praise for their work; they simply acted out of compassion and a fear of God, trusting that He would protect and bless them for their faithfulness. Their story is a powerful reminder that serving in the shadows can have a profound impact, even if it's not immediately visible or recognized by others. It's about persevering in our efforts to do what is right, even when it's hard, and trusting that God sees and values every act of service, no matter how hidden or small it may seem. Shiphrah and Puah's courageous and selfless service saved lives and helped shape the future of an entire nation, showing us that even the quiet, behind-the-scenes work of those who serve in the shadows can change the course of history.

Chapter 6 – The Skillful Steward

Bezalel, the skillful steward, serves as a powerful example of "serving in the shadows," as depicted in Exodus 35:30-35. His role as a craftsman wasn't one that involved standing in front of large crowds, delivering sermons, or leading armies into battle. Instead, he worked quietly behind the scenes, using the talents that God had given him to help build the tabernacle, the sacred place where the Israelites would come to worship God. Bezalel's story is a reminder that even when we are not in the spotlight, our service to God can have a profound and lasting impact. God chose Bezalel specifically because of his exceptional skill and wisdom in craftsmanship. The Bible tells us that God filled him with His Spirit, giving him the ability to work with gold, silver, bronze, stone, and wood, crafting everything from intricate designs to large structures. Bezalel didn't seek out glory or recognition for his work, but his craftsmanship was crucial to the creation of the tabernacle, where God's presence would dwell among His people. In this way, Bezalel's behind-the-scenes service helped facilitate the worship of God for generations to come.

What stands out about Bezalel's service is how he embraced the role that God gave him. He didn't seek to be someone he wasn't, but instead faithfully stewarded the gifts and talents that God had entrusted to him. His work was a form of worship in itself, using his skills to glorify God in a tangible way. By crafting the tabernacle with such precision and beauty, Bezalel helped create a sacred space where the Israelites could encounter God. Though he wasn't leading the people like Moses or Aaron, his contributions were just as important to the spiritual life of the nation. Bezalel's story teaches us that serving in the shadows doesn't mean our work is less valuable or less important. It means using our God-given abilities, whatever they may be, to contribute to the greater good of God's kingdom, even if we don't receive public recognition for it.

Bezalel's work also highlights the importance of excellence in everything we do for God. He wasn't just doing a job; he was creating something beautiful and meaningful that would reflect God's glory. His attention to detail, his dedication to craftsmanship, and his commitment to using his talents to the best of his ability are all examples of how we should approach the tasks that God gives us. Whether we are called to build, teach, serve, or lead, we should do everything with the same care and dedication that Bezalel showed in building the tabernacle. Serving in the shadows means giving our best effort, even when others may not notice, because we know that God sees and values our work.

Another important lesson from Bezalel's life is the idea of collaboration. Though Bezalel was the chief craftsman, he didn't work alone. God also gave him the wisdom to teach others, including Oholiab and other skilled craftsmen, so that they could work together to build the tabernacle. This shows us that serving in the shadows often involves working with others, sharing our knowledge, and helping those around us grow in their own abilities. Bezalel wasn't concerned with keeping all the glory for himself; he understood that the task God had given him was bigger than one person. By teaching others and working as part of a team, Bezalel helped ensure that the tabernacle would be completed according to God's design. His willingness to collaborate and share his skills reminds us that serving in the shadows is often about building others up and working together to achieve a common goal.

What makes Bezalel's story so compelling is that it shows us how God values every type of service, no matter how visible or hidden it may be. While some people are called to lead and others are called to preach, people like Bezalel are called to serve behind the scenes, using their unique talents to support the work of the ministry. Bezalel's work on the tabernacle may not have been as public as the work of Moses or Aaron, but it was no less important. The tabernacle was the place where God's presence would dwell, and Bezalel's craftsmanship played a key role in making that a reality. His work enabled the people of Israel to have a place to worship, to bring their sacrifices, and to encounter God's presence in their midst. In this way, Bezalel's service, though hidden from the spotlight, had a lasting impact on the spiritual life of the entire nation.

Bezalel's story also teaches us about the importance of stewardship. God gave Bezalel his skills, and Bezalel used those skills to serve God and His people. He didn't waste his talents or use them for selfish gain; he used them to fulfill God's purpose. This is a powerful reminder that everything we have—our talents, our time, our resources—comes from God, and it's our responsibility to use those gifts in a way that honors Him. Bezalel's faithful stewardship of his abilities shows us that serving in the shadows means being a good steward of what God has given us, no matter how big or small the task may seem. It's about recognizing that even the most mundane tasks, when done for the glory of God, have eternal significance.

In conclusion, Bezalel, the skillful steward, exemplifies what it means to serve in the shadows. Though his work as a craftsman was done behind the scenes, it was essential to the worship of God among the Israelites. Bezalel used his God-given talents to build the tabernacle, creating a space where God's presence could dwell and where the people could come to worship. His story reminds us that serving in the shadows is not about seeking recognition or glory, but about faithfully using the gifts that God has entrusted to us. Whether we are working in the background or in the spotlight, our service to God is valuable and important. Bezalel's attention to detail, his commitment to excellence, and his willingness to collaborate with others all show us how we can serve God with our best efforts, even when our work goes unnoticed by others. Ultimately, Bezalel's story teaches us that when we serve in the shadows, we are contributing to something much bigger than ourselves—God's kingdom—and that is a privilege and an honor.

Chapter 7 – The Supportive Son of Encouragement

Barnabas, known as the Supportive Son of Encouragement, is an inspiring example of serving in the shadows, as shown in Acts 4:36-37 and Acts 9:26-27. Barnabas wasn't someone who sought the spotlight or craved attention, but his actions played a critical role in the development of the early Christian church. His name, which means "Son of Encouragement," perfectly reflects his character and the way he served others. Barnabas had a gift for uplifting and supporting people, and his behind-the-scenes encouragement was essential to the success of many early church leaders, particularly Paul. When Paul, formerly known as Saul, first converted to Christianity, many of the believers were afraid of him because of his past as a persecutor of Christians. They didn't trust him, and it was hard for Paul to be accepted into the community of believers. But Barnabas stepped in to support Paul when no one else would. He stood by Paul's side and vouched for him, convincing the apostles that Paul's conversion was genuine. Barnabas's encouragement and belief in Paul were crucial at a time when Paul was still trying to find his footing in his new faith, and without Barnabas's support, Paul might never have become the influential leader we know today.

What makes Barnabas's service so remarkable is that he wasn't focused on getting credit for himself. He was happy to serve behind the scenes, offering support and encouragement to others so that they could thrive. In Acts 4:36-37, we learn that Barnabas sold a piece of land he owned and gave the money to the apostles to support the early church. This generous act was done quietly, without any desire for recognition or praise. Barnabas wasn't concerned with being in the spotlight; his main goal was to help the church grow and to support those who were working to spread the message of Jesus. His selflessness and generosity were hallmarks of his character, and they show us that serving in the shadows often means putting others before ourselves and being willing to make sacrifices for the greater good.

Barnabas's role in supporting Paul didn't stop with his initial introduction to the apostles. Later, when Paul began his missionary work, Barnabas accompanied him on several journeys, working alongside him to spread the gospel to new regions. Though Paul is often the one credited with the success of these missions, Barnabas's support was critical to their effectiveness. He wasn't interested in being the one in charge or getting all the attention; he was content to serve as a partner, helping Paul fulfill his calling and encouraging him along the way. This kind of humble service is what makes Barnabas such a powerful example of serving in the shadows. He understood that true leadership isn't about seeking glory for oneself, but about helping others succeed and lifting them up so that they can reach their full potential.

Barnabas also played a key role in encouraging and mentoring other early church leaders. In Acts 11, we see that Barnabas was sent to Antioch to help the new believers there grow in their faith. When he arrived, he saw the grace of God at work and was filled with joy. He encouraged the believers to remain true to the Lord, and his presence was a great source of strength and inspiration for them. But Barnabas didn't stop there. He recognized that the church in Antioch needed more help, so he went to find Paul and brought him to Antioch to assist in teaching and leading the new believers. Barnabas's willingness to seek out Paul and bring him into the work shows his deep commitment to building up others and ensuring that the church had the support it needed to thrive. He wasn't concerned with doing everything himself or being the center of attention; instead, he focused on bringing others into the fold and encouraging them to use their gifts to serve the church.

Another powerful aspect of Barnabas's service is that he was willing to give people second chances. In Acts 15:36-41, we see that Barnabas stood up for John Mark, who had previously abandoned Paul and Barnabas on a missionary journey. Paul didn't want to take John Mark with them on their next mission because of his earlier failure, but Barnabas believed in giving him another chance. This led to a disagreement between Paul and Barnabas, and they decided to go their separate ways, with Barnabas taking John Mark with him. Barnabas's decision to stand by John Mark shows his deep commitment to encouraging and supporting others, even when they had made mistakes. He saw potential in John Mark and was willing to invest in him, believing that he could still be useful to the work of the church. This act of support and encouragement had a lasting impact, as John Mark went on to become a valuable member of the early church and is traditionally believed to be the author of the Gospel of Mark.

Barnabas's story teaches us that serving in the shadows is about lifting others up, supporting them in their calling, and encouraging them to keep going, even when the road is tough. He wasn't interested in being the one in the spotlight; instead, he focused on helping others succeed. His actions remind us that true service is often quiet and unnoticed, but it is incredibly powerful. Barnabas didn't need recognition or praise for his work; he found joy in seeing others grow in their faith and in helping them fulfill their God-given potential. This kind of service requires humility, generosity, and a deep commitment to the well-being of others, all qualities that Barnabas exemplified.

In conclusion, Barnabas, the Supportive Son of Encouragement, shows us what it means to serve in the shadows. His behind-the-scenes work was critical to the growth of the early church, and his support of leaders like Paul and John Mark helped shape the future of Christianity. Barnabas's willingness to encourage and uplift others, even when he didn't receive recognition for his efforts, is a powerful reminder that serving in the shadows is just as important as leading from the front. His story challenges us to think about how we can serve others in quiet, meaningful ways, without seeking attention or praise. Like Barnabas, we can make a lasting impact by supporting, encouraging, and believing in others, helping them to fulfill their potential and contribute to the work of God's kingdom.

Chapter 8 – The Steadfast Supporter

Joanna, known as the steadfast supporter, is a remarkable example of serving in the shadows, as seen in Luke 8:3. She played a crucial but often overlooked role in the ministry of Jesus. Unlike many of the well-known figures in the Gospels, Joanna wasn't out in front preaching or performing miracles; instead, she quietly supported Jesus and His disciples in a different but equally important way—by providing financial support. Joanna's contributions were essential to sustaining Jesus' ministry, allowing Him and His disciples to travel, preach, and spread the message of the kingdom of God without worrying about basic needs like food and shelter. Even though her name is not mentioned as often as others, the impact of her steadfast service was undeniable. Her quiet dedication to supporting Jesus and His mission shows us that serving in the shadows, even in practical ways that may not seem as visible, can have a profound and lasting effect.

What makes Joanna's service so powerful is the humility and faithfulness with which she carried it out. She wasn't seeking recognition or praise for her support; she gave generously because she believed in the importance of Jesus' work and wanted to help in any way she could. In many ways, Joanna's financial support was the backbone of the ministry. Traveling across towns and cities, preaching to crowds, and caring for the needs of a group of disciples required resources, and Joanna's contributions helped make that possible. Though the Gospels don't provide many details about her personal life or her involvement beyond this, her role behind the scenes was critical. By providing financial backing, Joanna enabled the ministry to continue, making it possible for Jesus and His disciples to focus on teaching, healing, and spreading the Gospel message.

Joanna's actions remind us that serving in the shadows often means offering practical support that isn't always visible or celebrated. While others may have been in the spotlight, performing miracles or preaching to large crowds, Joanna's quiet generosity was equally vital. She understood that not every act of service needed to be front and center. Sometimes, the most important contributions happen behind the scenes, where no one is watching except God. Her willingness to give without seeking attention is a powerful example of true humility and devotion. Joanna didn't need to be in the limelight to know that her efforts mattered; she simply wanted to help Jesus in any way she could, trusting that her support was making a difference.

Another remarkable aspect of Joanna's service is the personal sacrifice it likely required. Financial support, especially at that time, wasn't always easy to come by, and for someone to give consistently to support a ministry like Jesus', it likely required significant commitment and personal cost. But Joanna didn't hesitate to give. Her steadfast support shows that serving in the shadows often involves sacrificing something of our own for the sake of others. Whether it's time, resources, or energy, serving in this way means being willing to put the needs of others before our own. Joanna's willingness to do this reminds us that service isn't always glamorous, but it is always valuable when it comes from a place of love and devotion.

Joanna's story also teaches us that even though her service may not have been highlighted or celebrated in the same way as others, it was still an essential part of God's plan. Jesus' ministry had many different aspects, from teaching and healing to traveling and caring for His disciples, and each part played a role in spreading the message of the kingdom. Joanna's financial support allowed these other parts to happen, showing us that every act of service, no matter how small or hidden, plays a role in God's greater purpose. Sometimes, it's easy to think that only the people who are visibly leading or teaching are making a difference, but Joanna's example proves that those who serve behind the scenes are just as important to the success of God's work.

Another important point in Joanna's story is her consistency. The Bible doesn't say that she supported Jesus and His disciples for just a short time or only when it was convenient. Her support was steadfast, meaning she was committed to helping them throughout their ministry. This kind of consistent service, even when it might have been challenging or required ongoing sacrifice, shows incredible dedication and faith. Serving in the shadows often means staying committed over the long haul, even when it's hard or when others might not notice what we're doing. Joanna's faithfulness in her support is a reminder that true service requires endurance and perseverance. It's about continuing to give, even when the recognition isn't there or when the task seems mundane.

In conclusion, Joanna, the steadfast supporter, is a powerful example of serving in the shadows through her quiet, faithful financial support of Jesus and His disciples. Though her contributions are not often highlighted in the Gospels, they were essential to sustaining the ministry, allowing Jesus and His followers to focus on spreading the message of God's kingdom. Joanna's story teaches us that serving in the shadows is just as important as serving in the spotlight. Her humble, consistent, and sacrificial support enabled the ministry to continue, showing us that even the quietest acts of service can have a profound and lasting impact. Whether we are serving by giving financially, offering practical help, or supporting others behind the scenes, Joanna's example reminds us that every act of service matters in God's eyes and plays a vital role in His greater plan.

Chapter 9 – The Servant of Paul

Onesimus, the servant of Paul, is an extraordinary example of serving in the shadows, as shown in Philemon 1:10-11. Onesimus was once a slave who, after his conversion to Christianity, became a valuable servant and companion to the Apostle Paul. Though his story is often overshadowed by other, more well-known figures in the Bible, Onesimus's life and service played a key role in the spread of the gospel and in fostering reconciliation among believers. Onesimus's journey began in a difficult place—he had been a slave, and according to the historical context, he ran away from his master, Philemon, possibly after committing some wrong. This action could have resulted in severe punishment in those times, but through God's grace, Onesimus encountered Paul while Paul was in prison. Paul shared the message of Jesus Christ with Onesimus, and this led to Onesimus's conversion. From that point on, Onesimus's life changed, and he began to serve Paul, not as a slave bound by chains, but as a brother in Christ, committed to the work of spreading the gospel.

What makes Onesimus's story so compelling is the way he embraced his new role as a servant of the gospel. His transformation from a runaway slave to a trusted companion of Paul speaks to the redemptive power of Christ. Although Onesimus's service took place behind the scenes and is only briefly mentioned in the Bible, it was essential to the early Christian mission. Paul himself recognized the importance of Onesimus's service, describing him as someone who had become "useful" in Philemon 1:11. In fact, Paul goes as far as to say that Onesimus was not just useful to him personally, but also useful to the work of the gospel, which shows the deep value Paul placed on Onesimus's contributions. Onesimus didn't seek the spotlight or public recognition for his efforts; instead, he faithfully served in whatever way he could, assisting Paul during his imprisonment and contributing to the spread of the Christian message.

Onesimus's story also illustrates the beauty of reconciliation and forgiveness within the Christian community. After Onesimus's conversion, Paul wrote a letter to Philemon, Onesimus's former master, asking Philemon to welcome Onesimus back, not as a slave, but as a brother in Christ. This act of reconciliation is a powerful aspect of Onesimus's story because it highlights how the gospel transforms relationships. In those times, the relationship between a master and a slave was one of power and control, but through the message of Jesus, Paul urged Philemon to see Onesimus not as property, but as a fellow believer and equal in the eyes of God. This request for reconciliation between Onesimus and Philemon shows how serving in the shadows can bring about profound changes in people's hearts and relationships. Onesimus's quiet service helped pave the way for a deeper understanding of Christian love, equality, and forgiveness among the early believers.

Even though Onesimus's story remains largely in the background, the lessons we can learn from his life are significant. Serving in the shadows, as Onesimus did, means working faithfully and humbly, even when others may not notice or acknowledge our efforts. It's about putting aside personal ambitions and focusing on the larger mission of spreading the gospel and serving others. Onesimus didn't need to be in the spotlight to make a difference; his willingness to serve Paul and the Christian community in whatever capacity he could was what made him valuable. His story shows us that God can use anyone, regardless of their past, to contribute to His kingdom. Onesimus had once been a slave, a person without freedom or rights, but through his faith and service, he became an important figure in the early church, demonstrating that our value to God is not determined by our past or our status, but by our willingness to serve Him.

Onesimus's service is also a testament to the power of transformation through Christ. Before his conversion, Onesimus may have felt like he was trapped by his circumstances, but after meeting Paul and accepting the gospel, he found a new purpose. His service to Paul was not a return to slavery, but a voluntary act of love and devotion to both Paul and the message of Jesus. This transformation from a runaway slave to a beloved brother in Christ shows how serving in the shadows can lead to personal growth and spiritual renewal. Onesimus didn't let his past define him; instead, he embraced the opportunity to serve in a new way, contributing to the spread of the gospel and helping to build the early church.

Furthermore, Onesimus's story reminds us that the impact of our service is not always immediately visible. While his name is not as prominent as Paul's or other apostles, Onesimus's quiet work behind the scenes played a crucial role in supporting Paul during his imprisonment and in maintaining the unity of the Christian community. By returning to Philemon and seeking reconciliation, Onesimus became an example of how the gospel can heal divisions and create new relationships built on mutual respect and love. His service, though hidden, had far-reaching consequences for the early church, as it helped to strengthen the bonds between believers and demonstrated the power of forgiveness and brotherhood in Christ.

In conclusion, Onesimus, the servant of Paul, exemplifies what it means to serve in the shadows. His life was transformed through his encounter with Paul and the message of Jesus, and he became a faithful servant to the gospel, working quietly behind the scenes to support Paul and help spread the Christian message. Onesimus's story teaches us that serving in the shadows requires humility, faithfulness, and a willingness to put the needs of others before our own. It shows us that God can use anyone, no matter their background or circumstances, to contribute to His kingdom. Onesimus's service also highlights the importance of reconciliation and forgiveness within the Christian community, as his return to Philemon symbolized the healing power of the gospel. Though his story may not be as well-known as others, the impact of Onesimus's service was profound, reminding us that even the most humble acts of service can play a vital role in God's plan.

Chapter 10 – The Silent Messenger

Tychicus, the silent messenger, is a powerful example of serving in the shadows, as described in Ephesians 6:21-22. Though his role in the early church might seem small compared to the more famous figures like Paul, Peter, or John, Tychicus played an essential part in the growth and unity of the early Christian community. His main responsibility was to serve as a messenger, delivering important letters from Paul to the various early churches. These letters weren't just ordinary correspondence—they contained teachings, encouragement, and guidance that would shape the beliefs and practices of Christians for generations to come. Paul's letters to the churches, including Ephesians, Colossians, and others, were crucial to the spiritual growth of these early believers, and without someone like Tychicus to faithfully carry these messages from city to city, the letters may never have reached their intended recipients.

Tychicus didn't seek attention or recognition for his work. He served quietly and faithfully, often behind the scenes, and his name isn't mentioned frequently in the New Testament. However, the few times he is mentioned show just how much trust Paul had in him. Paul referred to Tychicus as a "beloved brother" and a "faithful minister in the Lord," highlighting his deep character and reliability. Tychicus wasn't just someone who delivered letters—he was someone Paul trusted with critical responsibilities. Paul knew that Tychicus would not only deliver the letters but also provide the churches with updates about Paul's situation in prison and encourage them in their faith. Tychicus's willingness to travel long distances, often under difficult and dangerous conditions, to deliver these letters shows his dedication to serving the church, even when his service wasn't publicly recognized.

What makes Tychicus's service even more meaningful is that it wasn't just a one-time task. He consistently served as a messenger, traveling to multiple cities and regions to ensure that Paul's letters reached the early believers. His work helped maintain communication among the churches, which was vital for their unity and strength. At a time when there were no phones, emails, or quick forms of communication, someone like Tychicus was indispensable. His role ensured that the early Christians remained connected with one another and with Paul, who was imprisoned during much of this time. The messages he carried were not only practical but spiritual, helping to strengthen the faith of believers, instruct them in the ways of Christ, and address issues that arose in their communities. Without Tychicus, many of these letters, which now make up a significant portion of the New Testament, might not have been preserved or passed along, and the early church might have struggled to remain united and encouraged in the face of persecution and hardship.

Tychicus's story also teaches us an important lesson about the value of quiet, faithful service. In today's world, it's easy to think that only those who are in the spotlight—those who preach, lead, or perform miraculous acts—are truly making a difference. But Tychicus's example shows us that those who work behind the scenes, faithfully doing the tasks that others may overlook, are just as vital to the mission of God's kingdom. Tychicus didn't preach to large crowds or perform public miracles, but his work was crucial to the spread of the gospel. Serving in the shadows often means doing work that others may not notice, but that doesn't make it any less important. In fact, it's often these quiet, unseen acts of service that keep everything else running smoothly. Tychicus may not have been in the spotlight, but his faithfulness helped ensure that the gospel message continued to spread and that believers were encouraged and equipped to live out their faith.

Another remarkable aspect of Tychicus's service is the humility with which he carried out his work. He didn't seem to mind that his name wasn't well-known or that he didn't receive the same level of recognition as Paul or the other apostles. Tychicus was content to serve in the role that God had given him, knowing that his work was important, even if it wasn't as visible as that of others. This kind of humility is a key characteristic of serving in the shadows. It requires a willingness to set aside personal ambition and the desire for recognition, focusing instead on the needs of others and the mission of spreading the gospel. Tychicus's example shows us that true service isn't about seeking praise or attention—it's about being faithful to the work that God has called us to do, no matter how small or unnoticed it may seem.

Tychicus's service also involved a great deal of personal sacrifice. Traveling in the ancient world was not easy. It was often dangerous, with long, arduous journeys on foot or by sea, through difficult terrain, and with the constant threat of robbery or illness. Yet Tychicus willingly took on these challenges because he believed in the importance of the work he was doing. His willingness to endure hardship for the sake of the gospel is a powerful reminder that serving in the shadows often requires sacrifice. It's not always comfortable or convenient, but those who are willing to make those sacrifices help to further God's kingdom in ways that have a lasting impact. Tychicus wasn't focused on his own comfort or safety; he was committed to ensuring that Paul's letters reached the churches so that believers could be strengthened and encouraged.

Tychicus's role as a messenger also highlights the importance of being trustworthy and reliable in our service. Paul trusted Tychicus not only to deliver his letters but also to represent him to the churches and provide updates about his situation in prison. Tychicus's faithfulness in this role shows that serving in the shadows often means being someone who others can rely on, even when the work is difficult or unglamorous. Tychicus didn't let Paul down—he carried out his responsibilities with dedication and care, knowing that his work was essential to the spread of the gospel and the growth of the church. His story challenges us to think about how we can be faithful in the tasks God has given us, even when they seem small or go unnoticed by others. It reminds us that being dependable and trustworthy in our service is just as important as the work itself.

In conclusion, Tychicus, the silent messenger, exemplifies what it means to serve in the shadows. His quiet, faithful work behind the scenes was crucial to the growth and unity of the early church. By delivering Paul's letters and maintaining communication among the churches, Tychicus helped ensure that believers remained connected, encouraged, and instructed in their faith. Though his name is not often mentioned, his service had a profound impact on the spread of the gospel and the strength of the early Christian community. Tychicus's humility, reliability, and willingness to sacrifice for the sake of the gospel show us that serving in the shadows is not about seeking recognition or praise, but about being faithful to the work God has called us to do, no matter how small or unseen it may seem. His story challenges us to embrace the role of quiet service, trusting that even our hidden efforts can have a lasting impact on God's kingdom. Through Tychicus's example, we learn that those who serve behind the scenes are just as vital to the mission of spreading the gospel as those who are in the spotlight, and that every act of service, no matter how small, plays an important role in the growth of God's church.

Chapter 11 – The Silent Soldier

Jonathan's armor-bearer, the silent soldier, is an extraordinary example of serving in the shadows, as depicted in 1 Samuel 14:6-7. Although his name is never mentioned in the Bible, his loyalty, bravery, and quiet commitment played a critical role in one of Israel's most remarkable victories over the Philistines. In this passage, Jonathan, the son of King Saul, decides to take a bold and risky action against the Philistine army. Jonathan is confident that God can bring victory, whether He has many soldiers or just a few. He shares his plan with his armor-bearer, who doesn't hesitate or question him but responds with complete trust and loyalty. The armor-bearer says to Jonathan, "Do all that is in thine heart: turn thee; behold, I am with thee according to thy heart." This response shows the unwavering faithfulness of the armor-bearer, who is willing to follow Jonathan into a dangerous situation without any guarantee of success. His willingness to serve in such a quiet yet dangerous role demonstrates the strength of his character and his dedication to the mission, even though he remains in the background of the story.

What makes the armor-bearer's service so powerful is that it is done without any expectation of recognition or glory. He isn't the one making the bold decisions or leading the charge, but he plays an essential role by standing beside Jonathan and supporting him through the battle. His service highlights the importance of working in the background, doing the hard, unseen tasks that make success possible. Without the armor-bearer's readiness to follow Jonathan and fight by his side, the victory might not have been achieved. He wasn't seeking to make a name for himself or stand out as a hero, but his quiet courage and support were critical to the success of the mission. Serving in the shadows often means performing tasks that may not be noticed by others, but that doesn't mean those tasks are any less important. The armor-bearer's example reminds us that even those who aren't in the spotlight can have a significant impact through their faithfulness and dedication.

The armor-bearer's service is also a powerful demonstration of loyalty. He trusted Jonathan completely, not only in his leadership but also in his faith in God. Jonathan's plan to confront the Philistines was bold and dangerous, and from a human perspective, it seemed like a long shot. But Jonathan believed that God could give them victory, and the armor-bearer trusted both Jonathan and God enough to follow him into battle without hesitation. This kind of loyalty, both to a leader and to the mission at hand, is a hallmark of serving in the shadows. It requires humility and a willingness to set aside personal fears or desires in order to support someone else's vision. The armor-bearer's trust in Jonathan allowed him to step into a situation that was filled with risk, showing us that serving in the shadows often requires courage. It's not about receiving recognition or accolades; it's about faithfully doing what needs to be done, even when it's difficult or dangerous.

The armor-bearer's role also highlights the importance of partnership in service. Jonathan and his armor-bearer worked together as a team, with each one playing a crucial role in the battle. Jonathan may have been the one making the decisions, but the armor-bearer was right there with him, carrying his armor, fighting alongside him, and providing the support that Jonathan needed. This partnership between the two shows that serving in the shadows often involves working in collaboration with others, even if one person's role is more visible than the other's. The armor-bearer wasn't the one making the bold speeches or leading the charge, but without his presence and support, Jonathan wouldn't have been able to accomplish what he did. Their teamwork reminds us that in any mission or task, the roles that are less visible or less celebrated are just as important as the ones in the spotlight. True service requires everyone working together, with each person contributing in their own way, whether seen or unseen.

The bravery of Jonathan's armor-bearer is another important aspect of his service. Following Jonathan into battle against a much larger and more powerful enemy required immense courage. The armor-bearer didn't know what the outcome of the battle would be, and he had no guarantees of victory, but he trusted Jonathan's leadership and God's power. His willingness to face danger head-on, even though his role was more supportive than leading, shows that serving in the shadows often requires a deep sense of bravery. It's not about being in the spotlight or receiving recognition; it's about having the courage to do what is necessary, even when it's difficult or frightening. The armor-bearer's bravery didn't come from a desire for glory, but from his commitment to the mission and his trust in God's plan.

The fact that the armor-bearer remains unnamed throughout the story is also significant. In many ways, this highlights the humility that is often required in serving in the shadows. The armor-bearer didn't need his name to be recorded or celebrated in order to be faithful to his task. His focus wasn't on gaining recognition or fame; it was on supporting Jonathan and doing what was needed to secure victory for Israel. This kind of humility is a key aspect of serving in the shadows. It requires a willingness to set aside personal ambition and be content with playing a supporting role, knowing that the work being done is important, even if it goes unrecognized by others. The armor-bearer's willingness to remain in the background, without seeking attention or praise, is a powerful example of the kind of humble service that is so valuable in God's kingdom.

The victory that Jonathan and his armor-bearer achieved over the Philistines was a turning point in Israel's struggle against their enemies. Though the armor-bearer's name is not recorded, his quiet, faithful service contributed to this significant victory. His role may have been silent, but it was far from insignificant. The armor-bearer's example teaches us that serving in the shadows doesn't mean our work is less important. In fact, it's often the quiet, hidden acts of service that make the biggest difference in the long run. The armor-bearer's support of Jonathan allowed them to defeat the Philistines and helped bring about a great victory for Israel, showing us that even those who serve in the background can have a profound impact on the outcome of important events.

In conclusion, Jonathan's armor-bearer, the silent soldier, exemplifies the true spirit of serving in the shadows. His loyalty, bravery, and humility made him an invaluable part of Jonathan's mission, even though his name is not recorded and his actions remain largely unseen. By faithfully supporting Jonathan in battle, the armor-bearer played a crucial role in Israel's victory over the Philistines. His story reminds us that serving in the shadows requires loyalty, courage, humility, and a willingness to support others, even when we don't receive recognition for our efforts. The armor-bearer's example shows that those who serve quietly and faithfully, without seeking attention or praise, are often the ones who make the greatest impact. Though his name may not be known, the armor-bearer's service was essential to the success of Jonathan's mission, proving that serving in the shadows is not about being seen, but about being faithful to the task at hand, trusting that God sees and values every act of service, no matter how small or hidden it may be.

Chapter 12 – The Small Yet Significant Servant

Naaman's servant girl, though small and seemingly insignificant, serves as a profound example of "serving in the shadows," as illustrated in 2 Kings 5:2-3. This unnamed young girl, taken captive from Israel and brought into the household of Naaman, a powerful Syrian commander, might have been seen as nothing more than a servant. She had no status, no voice in society, and no obvious power. Yet her quiet faith and courage played a critical role in bringing about one of the most remarkable stories of healing and transformation in the Bible. Despite her lowly position and the fact that she was a foreign captive in a strange land, this servant girl did not allow her circumstances to keep her from speaking up when she saw a need. Naaman, her master, was suffering from leprosy, a disease that was not only painful but socially isolating, making him desperate for healing. Instead of keeping quiet or feeling bitter about her captivity, this small but significant servant showed immense compassion and bravery by suggesting that Naaman seek healing from the prophet Elisha in Israel. Her quiet recommendation, spoken with faith and humility, set into motion a series of events that would ultimately lead to Naaman's miraculous healing and his acknowledgment of the one true God.

What makes the servant girl's role so compelling is that, despite her young age and lowly position, she acted with remarkable wisdom and faith. She could have easily kept silent, thinking that someone like her—a young servant girl in a foreign land—had no influence or ability to change her master's situation. Yet she chose to speak up, demonstrating her deep belief in God's power to heal through His prophet Elisha. Her faith was unwavering, even though she lived in a land where people worshipped other gods. She didn't hesitate to point Naaman, a powerful military leader, to the prophet of her God, showing that she believed in God's ability to bring healing regardless of the circumstances. This quiet confidence in God's power is a key part of what it means to serve in the shadows. It's about having the faith to act, even when it seems like our role is small and unnoticed. The servant girl's willingness to share what she knew, despite her position, teaches us that no matter how insignificant we may feel, God can use our faith and actions to bring about incredible change.

The servant girl's suggestion was not only bold, but it also came at great personal risk. As a captive servant, speaking out of turn or giving advice to her master could have been met with harsh consequences, especially if Naaman had been offended by her suggestion to seek help from an Israelite prophet. Yet this young girl's quiet courage is what makes her story so powerful. She didn't let fear or the potential for rejection stop her from offering the solution that she knew could bring healing. In this way, she shows us that serving in the shadows often requires bravery, even when our actions go unnoticed by most people. It's not about seeking recognition or fame, but about doing what is right, even when there is personal risk involved. Her courage in speaking up, despite her status, reminds us that even those who seem small or insignificant by the world's standards can make a huge difference when they act with faith and conviction.

Another important aspect of the servant girl's story is her compassion. Even though she had been taken from her home and was living as a servant in a foreign land, she didn't harbor bitterness or resentment toward Naaman or his household. Instead, she showed kindness and concern for her master's well-being. This compassion led her to offer the solution to Naaman's suffering, even though it would have been easy for her to remain silent or indifferent. Her ability to rise above her difficult circumstances and focus on helping others is a powerful example of what it means to serve in the shadows. Serving in the shadows often requires us to put aside our own struggles or feelings of insignificance in order to help others. The servant girl didn't let her situation define her; instead, she used her position to bring hope and healing to someone in need.

What makes the servant girl's service even more remarkable is that her small act of faith had far-reaching consequences. When Naaman followed her advice and went to see Elisha, he was miraculously healed of his leprosy after dipping in the Jordan River seven times, as Elisha had instructed. This healing was not only a physical miracle, but it also led to Naaman's spiritual transformation. After his healing, Naaman returned to Elisha and declared that he now knew that there was no God in all the earth except the God of Israel. This declaration of faith from a foreign military leader was a powerful testimony to the power of God, and it all began with the quiet words of a young servant girl. Her small, faithful act of pointing Naaman to Elisha had a ripple effect, leading to a miraculous healing and a public acknowledgment of God's greatness. This shows us that serving in the shadows can have a profound impact, even when we don't see the full results of our actions right away. The servant girl's story reminds us that God can use even the smallest acts of service to accomplish great things.

The fact that the servant girl remains unnamed in the Bible is also significant. Like many who serve in the shadows, she didn't receive public recognition or fame for her actions. Yet her story has been preserved for generations as an example of faith, courage, and quiet service. Her willingness to act without seeking credit or attention is a powerful reminder that serving in the shadows is not about being in the spotlight, but about being faithful to what God has called us to do, even when it goes unnoticed by others. The servant girl's example shows us that God sees and values every act of service, no matter how small or hidden it may be. Though she remains unnamed, her impact is undeniable, and her story continues to inspire people to this day.

In conclusion, Naaman's servant girl, the small yet significant servant, embodies what it means to serve in the shadows. Though she was young, unnamed, and in a position of low status, her faith, courage, and compassion played a pivotal role in Naaman's healing and spiritual transformation. Her quiet act of pointing Naaman to the prophet Elisha led to a miraculous healing and a public acknowledgment of the one true God. The servant girl's story teaches us that no matter how small or insignificant we may feel, God can use us in powerful ways when we act with faith and courage. Serving in the shadows requires humility, bravery, and a willingness to step out in faith, even when our actions go unnoticed by others. The servant girl's example shows that even the smallest acts of service can have far-reaching consequences and that God values and honors those who serve quietly and faithfully. Her story reminds us that serving in the shadows is not about seeking recognition, but about trusting that God can use our actions to bring about His purposes, even when we don't fully see the impact of our service.

Conclusion

As we conclude "Serving in the Shadows," we are reminded of the deep and lasting significance of serving faithfully, even when the world doesn't notice or acknowledge our efforts. Throughout this book, we've explored the stories of numerous individuals from the Bible who served quietly and humbly, using their God-given talents and faith to contribute to God's greater plan. Each of these individuals, whether it was Bezalel, who meticulously crafted the tabernacle, or Andrew, who brought his brother Peter to Jesus, teaches us the powerful truth that our value in God's kingdom is not measured by how much recognition we receive, but by our obedience, faithfulness, and love in the work we do. Serving in the shadows is not about seeking praise or being in the spotlight; it is about understanding that God sees our efforts, even when others do not, and that He values the heart of a servant more than the applause of people. As Christians, this understanding should shape how we live and continue to serve, motivating us to focus on God's glory and His will, rather than our own desire for attention or success.

Moving forward, it is essential to hold on to the lessons learned from these biblical examples. Just like Jonathan's armor-bearer, who remained loyal and brave without expecting any recognition, we, too, are called to serve with steadfastness and humility, knowing that our service is part of something much bigger than ourselves. Our lives, like those who have come before us, are meant to contribute to God's kingdom, even if our role is behind the scenes. This doesn't diminish the importance of what we do—it magnifies it, because God uses every act of service, no matter how small, to fulfill His plans. Whether we are caring for others, sharing the gospel, or simply loving people through acts of kindness, we are participating in the work of God, who takes our humble offerings and turns them into something extraordinary. We may never see the full impact of our service during our lifetime, but we can trust that God is working through us in ways we cannot imagine.

Serving in the shadows requires perseverance, especially when we feel overlooked or unappreciated. The world often encourages us to seek recognition and validation from others, but as Christians, our validation comes from God alone. He calls us to stay the course, to continue serving with a heart full of love and faith, even when it feels like no one is watching. This perseverance is rooted in the knowledge that God is always watching, and He delights in our faithfulness. It's easy to become discouraged when we feel like our work goes unnoticed, but the stories in this book remind us that nothing is wasted in God's kingdom. Every prayer, every act of kindness, every moment of quiet service is seen by God, and He promises to reward those who serve Him with pure hearts. As Paul encourages in Galatians 6:9, "And let us not be weary in well doing: for in due season we shall reap, if we faint not." This means that even when the work is hard, even when we feel tired or discouraged, we must continue to trust in God's timing and His faithfulness.

Another key to continuing in our service is humility. Each person we've studied in this book exemplified humility in their service. Bezalel didn't seek fame for his craftsmanship; instead, he used his skills to honor

God by building the tabernacle. Naaman's servant girl didn't seek glory for pointing her master to the prophet Elisha; she simply wanted to help. These examples remind us that true service comes from a place of humility, where we are not seeking our own advancement but are focused on advancing God's kingdom. When we serve with humility, we are free from the burden of trying to impress others or gain recognition. Instead, we find joy in knowing that we are fulfilling God's purpose for our lives, whether anyone else notices or not. Humility allows us to serve with genuine love and dedication, keeping our focus on God and His glory, rather than our own.

As Christians, continuing to serve in the shadows also means trusting in God's plan, even when we don't understand it fully. Often, we may not see the immediate results of our service, and it can be easy to question whether our efforts are making a difference. But just like the unnamed people in the Bible who played crucial roles in God's story, we must trust that God is using us in ways we cannot see. The servant girl in Naaman's story didn't know that her small act of speaking up would lead to Naaman's healing and eventual acknowledgment of God's power. Similarly, we may not always see how God is using our acts of service, but we can be confident that He is working through us for His purposes. Isaiah 55:8-9 reminds us, "For my thoughts are not your thoughts, neither are your ways my ways, saith the Lord. For as the heavens are higher than the earth, so are my ways higher than your ways, and my thoughts than your thoughts." God's ways are beyond our understanding, and that is why we must trust Him completely, knowing that He will bring about His perfect will through our service, even when we cannot see the full picture.

Furthermore, as we continue to serve in the shadows, it is essential to rely on God's strength rather than our own. One of the most significant challenges of serving without recognition is the emotional and physical exhaustion that can accompany it. We can become weary, frustrated, and even resentful when it feels like no one is noticing our efforts. But this is where our reliance on God becomes critical. In Isaiah 40:29, we are reminded that "He giveth power to the faint; and to them that have no might he increaseth strength." When we are tired, God renews our strength. When we feel unseen, God reminds us that He sees. When we are discouraged, God lifts our spirits. Continuing to serve in the shadows means acknowledging that we cannot do it on our own, but through God's strength, we can persevere and continue to make a difference.

Ultimately, serving in the shadows is about living a life of faith, obedience, and love. It is about being faithful to the calling that God has placed on our lives, regardless of whether or not the world notices. It is about being obedient to God's Word, knowing that He calls us to serve others as Christ served us. And it is about loving others selflessly, following the example of Jesus, who "came not to be ministered unto, but to minister, and to give his life a ransom for many" (Mark 10:45). Our service is an outpouring of the love we have received from God, and it is through that love that we can continue to serve with joy, even when our work goes unnoticed by the world.

In conclusion, as we close this book, let us be encouraged by the examples of those who served in the shadows. Let us continue to serve faithfully, with humility, perseverance, and trust in God. Let us remember that our worth is not measured by how many people recognize our efforts, but by our faithfulness to God's call. We may not always see the impact of our service, but God is using us in ways that are beyond our understanding. Every act of service, no matter how small, is part of His greater plan. So, as you continue your journey of serving in the shadows, know that you are not alone. God sees you, He values you, and He is working through you to accomplish His purposes. Your service matters, and in God's eyes, it is precious. Keep serving, keep loving, and keep trusting in Him, knowing that your work is making an eternal difference in the kingdom of God.

Don't miss out!

Visit the website below and you can sign up to receive emails whenever Joshua Rhoades publishes a new book. There's no charge and no obligation.

https://books2read.com/r/B-A-AJLBB-JNRBF

BOOKS 2 READ

Connecting independent readers to independent writers.

Did you love *Serving In The Shadows*? Then you should read *The Shout That Stopped The Saviour*[1] by Joshua Rhoades!

[2]

"The Shout That Stopped The Saviour" explores the remarkable story of Blind Bartimaeus, whose faith and desperation moved Jesus to perform one of the most memorable miracles in the Gospels. Mark 10:46-52 tells of a blind beggar whose cry for mercy halted Jesus on His journey, leading to a life-changing encounter. Bartimaeus' story goes beyond a physical healing; it illustrates the power of persistent faith, the importance of boldness in adversity, and the deep compassion Jesus has for those who seek Him earnestly.

In Jericho, Bartimaeus sat by the roadside, marginalized and overlooked, with only a desperate plea to offer. When he heard that Jesus of Nazareth was passing by, he didn't hesitate. Despite the crowd's attempts to silence him, Bartimaeus cried out louder, "Jesus, thou Son of David, have mercy on me!" This was no ordinary shout—it was a

---

1. https://books2read.com/u/b5DdNk

2. https://books2read.com/u/b5DdNk

cry from the depths of his soul, recognizing Jesus as the Messiah and pleading for mercy from the only One who could truly change his circumstances.

Bartimaeus' unwavering faith and determination in the face of opposition stand out. He wasn't discouraged by his status or blindness but saw with the eyes of faith what others could not—that Jesus had the power to heal and transform his life. His shout was an act of faith that stopped Jesus in His tracks.

"The Shout That Stopped The Saviour" invites readers to reflect on their own cries for help and expressions of faith in desperation. Bartimaeus' story challenges us to consider whether we, too, are willing to cry out to Jesus with boldness and persistence. It reminds us that Jesus hears the sincere cries of those who seek Him and responds with compassion and power, offering an invitation to experience the same transformative faith in our own lives.